THE SPIRITUAL POWER OF SALT

How to Use this Prayer Ritual for Financial
Abundance, Protection Against Witches, and
Get What You Want.

Gedaliah Shay

Alpha Zuriel Publishing

Should you not know that the Lord God of Israel
gave the dominion over Israel to David forever,
to him and his sons, by a covenant of salt?

— 2 CHRONICLES 13:5

CONTENTS

INTRODUCTION

Salt has an esoteric value as a symbol of purity in religious rituals. Early Greek worshippers glorified salt in their ancient customs; for instance, the Vestal Virgins sprinkled all propitiatory animals with salt and flour. Salt was a symbol of continuity to both Jews of the Old Testament and the New Testament Christians.

Salt has sustained both its cultural and religious pertinence due to its immense value and recognition in the ancient world for over three millennia or more.
Salt was approved for its importance as a prophylaxis to a food additive in the ancient pre-rationalist world. It has turned into a religious emblem, standing for immutability and ethical purity.

In Japan, for example, salt is considered a purifier. It is sprinkled on their doorstep after having an unwanted or distasteful guest.

To the Jews, it came to imply the never-ending covenant between Jews and Israel. Jewish temple atonement yet incorporates salt on the Sabbath, and orthodox Jews even drop their bread in salt to retain those sacrifices.

Treaties in both the Old and New Testaments were frequently sealed with salt, demonstrating the origin of the word "salvation." In the Catholic Church, salt is used in a variation of purging rituals. Jesus described his disciples "the Salt of the Earth," a narrative honored by the Catholic Church until Vatican II, by putting a small taste of salt on a baby's mouth at his or her rebirth.

In many beliefs, salt is still included on the altar to represent purity, and it is infused into the holy water of various sects for the same reason.

To the more orthodox Christians, salt continues to be a supernatural symbol of the permanent sacredness of Jesus and gives a supposed hands-on shield from evil. Salt is still utilized to make holy water and the more efficacious blessed water of the Roman Catholic Church.

In the center of the last millennia in Europe, salt remained deemed to produce security against witches, witchcraft, demons, and sprites. It was a general belief that witches, and the animals they enthralled, could not eat anything salted.

Demonologists recommended an amulet of salt for protection, consecrated on Palm Sunday, along with other blessed items, placed into a plate of blessed wax. No one can deny the power of salt either locally in food, benefits to the health, but not many are aware of its spiritual significance to men's lives even though it has long been in existence.

Many are ignorant concerning the spiritual uses and salt's power in getting what you want in prayers. It can be seen clearly in the scriptures' pages how the ancient men used salt in different spiritual aspects to strange birth results, and it still giving the same great results today.

There are several instances where salt the scripture mentioned salt both in the old and new testament. While salt may signify a bad omen, it's also positive signs applied in different ways.

One of the examples by Prophet Elisha "The men in the city told Elisha, "Look, our lord, this town is well situated, but our water is bad, and the land is unproductive." "Bring me a new bowl, "and put the salt inside it," Elisha instructed them. The men brought the bowl to him. He went to the spring and sprinkled the salt inside it and said, "This is what the LORD says 'I have healed the water and never again will it cause death or make the land unproductive" And the water has remained wholesome to this day, according to the word Elisha had spoken. (2 Kings 2:19-22).

In the above scripture, we could see how salt birthed a new reality through its application, from the water's healing to spiritual purification to preserve the territory where Elisha was the prophet.

There are diverse ways Jesus spoke to His disciples, relating them with salt, further showing how spiritually significant salt is and its connection with the believer's life; Many have suffered due to ignorance.

Traditionally, salt is well recognized for its spiritual uses as well. So, salt gives results according to your level of belief and not necessarily because you serve God. But what gives it more strength to deliver results is the prayer of faith and the declaration of God's powerful word as Christians.

There are several occasions where many use salt as one of the ingredients for prayers. They believe salt signifies sweetness, and if used in prayers, the individual will experience sweetness all the days of his life.

The powers of salt can be used to invite positive energies, such as those of wealth and prosperity. And old saying goes:

> *"May you always have salt at home, and may you always have money in your pocket."*

This book will enlighten you on salt's spiritual significance in prayers and its usage in prayer to get all you desire to get. The secrets in this book will cause liberation and enhance your prayer life as you pray in new dimensions with an extraordinary insight level.

CHAPTER ONE

THE DOMESTIC USES OF SALT

Naturally, salt works in diverse ways for man. Its health benefits and the ability to add taste and flavor to food is distinct and well recognized for decades. It is why salt is indispensable. Here are the ways salt we could use salt naturally in food.

Stomach ache

Salt is often mixed with warm water to control stomach ache locally. In homes, the first item women use for conditions like stomach ache is salt. It is believed that stomach ache occurs due to a rise in the stomach environment's acidic level, and when salt is used with warm water, it neutralizes it, and the stomach ache or upset subsides.

In food

Salt is well-known for its peculiar role as a flavoring agent and as a food preservative. Here are a few of the functional features of salt in food production.

Curing meat with salt is one of the oldest food preservation methods before discovering the refrigeration method. Microbes that spoil food require moisture to catalyze their growth; salt acts as a preservative by drawing water from the food particles. Many microbes that also cause different diseases are made lifeless due to the application of salt. It creates a level of concentration that makes that environment not suitable for their habitations.

Brine is a term used in food preservation when you mix salt with water for food preservation. It is the process of soaking food in salted water to preserve and make the food tasty. One example of brining is prickling.

Texture Influencer

When baking yeast bread, the amount of salt dramatically impacts the final texture of the bread. Salt alters the protein structure and the interaction of proteins with other components (e.g., water, fat, proteins), impacting foods' texture.

Most people are ignorant about the role of salt in giving food a fine texture. When baking yeast bread, salt dramatically affects yeast fermentation and gluten formation; they significantly affect the bread's final texture.

Salt also profoundly affects the gelatinization of proteins that happens during cheese production, and other processed meat examples include sausage and ham.

If the steak is well salted, the amount of liquid the meat will give will increase, giving it a more enjoyable taste. For a more crunchy texture, larger salt crystals are used to form soft and hard pretzels.

Flavor Alteration

Many often desire that foods have a "salty" flavor, but salt can also enhance other flavors, such as savory notes. It balances sweetness and helps suppress different tastes, such as bitterness.

Salt acts in different ways to enhance the flavor of food. Not only does it create a "salty" flavor element, one of the most desired tastes by humans, but salt can also affect other flavors, such as sweet and bitter.

The salt will intensify sweetness in small amounts, so it is sometimes sprinkled on fresh fruit or added to candies like cara-mel. It also normalizes some flavors' bitterness in food in the process known as "de-bitter," especially some cruciferous vegetables (including broccoli) and ol-ives.

Salt also ensures that certain important molecules are released inside the food to bring out the flavors of some added in-gredients inside the food.

Nutritional Content.

Salt contains sodium and chlorine ele-ments, essential nutrients needed by the body in large amounts.

Binding Agent

When salt is added to processed meats, the protein structures change as emulsi-fying and binding agents. The newly formed protein structure helps to hold the product together and prevent mois-ture and fat loss.

Bakery

Salt influences chemical reactions in food chemical reactions, including its ability to control yeast and dough development's fermentation rate. Salt increases the strength of the dough texture and makes it tighter. It impacts the shelf life of baked goods as it relates to water activity. Salt plays a flavor role in cereals and provides a texture and flavor-enhancing function in crackers.

Dairy/Cheese

Salt enhances the cheeses' flavor and preserves them when added. Many do not know this, while many professionals are aware of this technique in preserving cheese.

Salt interacts with milk protein to give an essential water-binding function.

CHAPTER TWO

BEST TYPES OF SALT FOR RITUALS

Many different types of salt can be used; some of these are:

Pink Himalayan Salt

Himalayan crystal salt is derived from salt mines 5,000 feet below the range of Himalayan Mountain. Its purity level is 99% because the salts experience a high amount of pressure in the mines. Due to the high mineral contents in Himalayan salt, it has varying colors. The crystal salt can be pink, white, or red. Some of its uses are:

Mineral Absorption

Skin is our largest organ in the entire body; it will absorb anything you put on it. Pink Himalayan salt contains over 84 minerals like calcium, magnesium, potassium, copper, and iron. Those minerals will soak right into the body through the skin.

Detoxification

We are exposed largely to toxins and chemicals every day through the food we eat, the inhaled air, and the water we drink and use. A pink salt bath is an excellent way to remove those chemicals from the skin.

Soothing

A warm bath with Himalayan pink added to the water is also great for relieving cramped muscles and inflammation reduction. The magnesium and some other minerals required in the body in high quality and found in the salt absorb through the skin to heal damaged muscles and other soft tissues in the body part. Minerals in pink salt also protect bones, skin, and connective tissues that may contribute to body soreness.

Deep Cleansing

Salt has antibacterial and antiseptic features that cleanse and also heal wounds, especially fresh ones. When conditions such as eczema, acne, or psoriasis help clearing them and cleaning them from the inside for healing to manifest. It also enhances blood circulation improvement. The salted bath helps avoid skin wrinkling as the salt increases the water retention of the skin and increases its hydration capacity to prevent dryness.

Epsom Salt

It contains a high mineral compound with magnesium with sulfate without the sodium chloride, the typical blend every ordinary salt must-have, especially the table salt. Epsom salt is magnesium bonded to sulfur and oxygen and, as such, not a salt. It softens the skin, detoxifies the body, relaxes sore muscles, and helps to reduce stress.

Dead Sea Salt

It has several healing features from the minerals contained in the salts. It strengthens the cell membranes, helps cleanses pores, and helps cells nourishment retainment. It functions in detoxification as well. Having a bath with dead sea salt solution sustains skin moisture and keeps the skin re-energized.

Dead Sea salt baths also help eliminate the roughness and inflammation on the skin's surface because of the high magnesium content. It also helps in the body's detoxification by removing the toxins through the pores while also improving blood circulation.

CHAPTER THREE

MEANING OF SALT FROM THE SCRIPTURE

Covenant relationships.

In ancient customs, men used salt to establish a bond of friendship through the eating of salt. They said if a man ate his friend's salt noted, you would become his friend for life. God desired that every sacrifice become a reminder of this desired relationship with us.

The emphasis of salt signifying relationship or covenant is also seen in Numbers 18 when Moses conversed with the priests concerning the covenant God made with them. Numbers 18:19 says,

> *"Whatever is set aside from the holy offerings the Israelites present to the Lord, I will give to you, your sons and daughters as your everlasting inheritance.*

It is an everlasting covenant of salt made before the Lord for you and your offspring."

2 Chronicles 13:5 talks about King David and the covenant of salt God made with him.

> *"Do you not perceive that the Lord God of Israel gave the kingdom over Israel to David permanently, even to him and his sons by a covenant of salt?"*

Ezekiel's 43:23 also shows us what salt signified in his book

> *"When you have purified it, you must give a young bull and a ram from the flock, both without blemish. You are to give them before the Lord, and the priests are to sprinkle salt on them and sacrifice as a burnt offering to the Lord."*

It was a reminder to Ezekiel and the priests of God's lasting commitment to his people.

When God requested that salt should be part of their grain offering, it was for a common reason. It has a deep meaning that revealed the relationship God desired to have with his people and how God desired his people to be the earth's preservative.

Influence

In the new testament, Jesus referred to believers to be salt and light while He was yet with His disciples.

> Matthew 5:13 "You are the salt of the earth. But if the salt should lose its saltiness, how can it be made salty again? It is no longer good for anything but to be discarded and trampled underfoot."

Jesus was telling His disciples how valuable and influential they are, their roles in the world to add value and meaning to others' lives, how they are always to replace people's bitterness with sweetness when men encounter them. It talks about the flavor men should add to the world even though the disciples didn't understand all His parables and metaphoric speeches till Jesus left the earth.

Moreover, He emphasized how important it was to retain their sweetness and flavor in life; if not, men would trample them under the foot. It is what happens when men lose their salvation, and their lives begin to go sour.

The reality is Jesus was showing them that the fact that He is with them shows how meaningful their lives are, and without His presence, their lives would lose their wonders, and men would see how worthless a man is without Christ.

Jesus knew how potent salt is, and He saw that was the most suitable metaphor to depict how meaningful a believer should live his life if Jesus could use salt to symbolize that, how potent it will be when applied in prayers to answer our prayer requests. Jesus answers our prayers if it is according to His will, and it is following His word.

Matt 5:13 is a powerful scripture that should be an anchor scripture for every believer. We must maintain our salt and all the great things God has done in and through our lives. A salted life is a seasoned life, and it must not be anything different from that.

Lot's wife's story is an excellent example for us in Genesis 19: 23-26. She changed to a pillar of salt because She looked back when the instruction given to them was to move forward following instructions and never look back to the sinful and rotten lives from which the Lord had saved them.

Genesis 19:23-26 "23,

"The sun had risen upon the earth when Lot entered into Zoar.

24 Then the Lord rained brimstone and fire out of heaven on Sodom and Gomorrah;25 He overthrew the cities, the plains, the inhabitants of the cities, and that which grew upon the ground. 26 But his wife looked back from behind him, and she became a pillar of salt."

The stories in the old testament often explain the new testament. While explaining the kingdom to us using parables in the scripture, Jesus told us that whoever dips his hands in the plow and looks back is not fit for the domain.

Lot's wife turned to salt due to her disobedience. That was the first and only place we saw a human being turning to salt due to noncompliance. I mean, when we disobey the Lord and go against His word and laws, our lives begin to lose their savor, meaning, sweetness. That was what happened to her.

Mark 9:42-50

"Whoever causes one of these little ones who believe in me to sin, it would be better for him if a great millstone were hung around his neck and he were thrown into the sea. 43 And if your hand causes you to sin, cut it off; it is better to t should enter life maimed than with two hands to go to hell, to the unquenchable fire. 45 And if your foot causes you to sin, cut it off; you should enter life lame than with two feet to be thrown into hell. 47 And if your eye causes you to sin, pluck it out; you should enter the kingdom of God with one eye than with two eyes to be thrown into hell, 48 where their worm does not die, and the fire is not quenched. 49 For everyone will be salted with fire. 50 Salt is good; but if the salt has lost its saltness, how will you season it? Have salt in yourselves, and be at peace with one another."

The passage speaks of sin and Jesus's temptation, giving us a stern warning to never go near sinful acts. In Mark 9:49, it shows how everyone's life will be salted with fire. It means that most believe fire represents trials and tribulations of life. It means that the people of God, as far as you are created by God and not just believers, will be salted or presented with issues and trials in life. These issues, problems, and difficulties are what bring sweetness and flavor to our lives. It is what trains us to be good soldiers of Christ, and outside Him, there is no victory.

Often, we pass through certain situations we cannot explain how we got there, why we had to pass through those trials and difficulties. Still, the truth is before salt ever become this valuable, and it passed through several stages of refining. Through several purification processes, just like gold would as well pass through that.

It is the reason why we must understand the Love of God that no matter what we pass through in this world, we can be bent but not destroyed. The transformation process is painful, and without the transformation process, man will remain in a sinful state and never have the power to exploit his life.

Salted life is a transformed life—one whose life is a reflection of Christ and His work. Salvation does not just stop when you access Christ as your Lord and savior. There is something called soul salvation, which is how our mind and soul are transformed to live a better, seasoned, and meaningful life as designed by God through the Holy Spirit.

Colossians 4:2-6

> *"2 Devote yourselves to prayer, being watchful, and thankful. 3 And pray for us, too, that God may open a door for our message, so that we may proclaim the mystery of Christ, for which I am in chains. 4 Pray that I may proclaim it clearly, as I should. 5 Be wise in the way you act toward outsiders; make the most of every opportunity. 6 Let your conversation be always full of grace, seasoned with salt, so that you may know how to answer everyone".*

From verse 6 of that scripture, salt simply signifies the life of a believer succinctly. If you have had a genuine encounter with God and have a strong relationship with the Holy Ghost, then a meeting with, you must leave a mark on other people's lives. You must leave them wanting for more of you because your life is seasoned with salt, full of grace, and the embodiment of love. Nothing should stop you from being who you should be from the eyes of God to the world.

Being seasoned with salt as a believer also speaks about the unique character of a believer. Many believers possess no virtue, and you keep wondering if they ever know Christ or serve Him. One fundamental truth is that our close walk with God should make His personality rub off on us. The scripture says we are transformed into His image as we behold Him; this is how our character is changed.

The uniqueness of our character is proof that we are truly serving God. According to the book of James, any life that is not seasoned with salt and grace cannot bring glory to God because it doesn't represent who He is. Our labor in prayers and bible study is what transforms our character.

The one reason why many believers' lives are not as described here is that we think staying in the world means communing with the world. The earth is our platform to showcase Christ, touch lives, transform them, and make them see the reasons why they need Jesus as their Lord and Savior of their souls.

Salt symbolizes a deep relationship God desire to have with us and how He wants us to preserve the earth and flavor it for Him. That is the mandate given to us in Genesis 1:28 that we should subdue the earth through our character's influence. Virtue is a weapon if developed diligently.

Salt is used in seasoning food
Job 6:6

> "Can that which is tasteless be eaten without salt, or is there any taste in the juice of the mallow."

Men used it in the scripture to season fodder in Isaiah 30:24 ", and the oxen and the donkeys that work the ground will eat the seasoned food. It shows how crucial salt can be. Although scripture is not to be interpreted most times, it could have several meanings.

In Leviticus 2:13,

> *"You shall season all your grain offerings with salt and shall not let the salt of the covenant with God be missing from your grain offering."*

It shows how seasoning offerings, especially grain offerings in the old testament signifies a covenant with God.

In the old testament, works and activities show your level of commitment with God; offerings and sacrifices show how deeply they love God and worship. God gave them instructions through the prophets on how they should present all their sacrificial offerings. It is incredible how salt could depict an everlasting covenant with God.

Ezra 4:14

> *"We have maintenance from the king's palace;" "We are salted with the salt of the palace;" "We eat the salt of the palace."*

Partaking in salted king's food in the old testament shows their level of hospitality and their relevance.

Numbers 18:*19*

> *"All the heave offerings of the holy things, which the children of Israel offer to the Lord, I have given to you and your sons and daughters with you as an ordinance forever; it is a covenant of salt forever before the Lord with you and your descendants with you."*

It is emphasizing on the covenant of salt between God and man.

The power of salt in enacting a long-lasting relationship between God and man has been in existence for ages. Today, offerings and sacrifices have been replaced with the sacrificial death of Jesus Christ once and for everyone.

2 Chronicle 13:5

> *"Should you not know that the Lord God of Israel gave the dominion over Israel to David permanently, to him and his sons, by a covenant of salt?".*

It shows the inheritance a man can get in the old testament through the covenant salt. David became a king and the lasting promise that his children will forever be on the throne as long as the covenant keeps speaking.

Salt was typically rubbed on every new-born baby, then

> *"On the day you were born your cord was not cut, nor were you washed with water to make you clean, nor were you rubbed with salt or wrapped in cloths" Ezekiel 16:4.*
>
> *Judges 9: 45," And all that day Abimelech fought against the city until he had captured it and killed its people. Then he demolished the city and sowed it with salt"*

Abimelech took over the city of Shechem, he sowed the seed of salt, that it should remain barren forever as salt connotes covenant that lasts forever.

Based on scientific inquiries, Sir Lyon Playfair argued that the generic name of "salt," in some specific passages, connotes petroleum or its residue asphalt. Thus, it means in Genesis 19:26 "But Lot's wife looked back, and she became a pillar of salt," it should read "pillar of asphalt;" and also in Matthew 5:13 "You are the salt of the earth. But if the salt loses its saltiness, how can it be made salty again? It is no longer good for anything, except to be thrown out and trampled underfoot". Instead of "salt," "petroleum," which its significance is lost when exposed to air as salt does, and becomes asphalt, with which they constructed the pavements.

There are different meanings of salt from the scripture. While many believe salt represents desolation looking at the story of Lot's wife in Genesis 19 where she turned to salt, many still hold on to that belief system that salt is a potent weapon in fighting off certain things that are demonic in life and also for restoration of lost opportunities, jobs, etc. in life.

In Leviticus, the Mosiac law reveals how the freewill offering preparation involves people coming with salt to show a promise. It includes unleavened bread, birds, goats, sheep, and cattle.

But aside from the fact that salt was a symbol of a covenant, this mineral was often an essential part of the offering because it was an expensive and highly valued item.

Salt was used in the scripture to show the covenant between God and man. A covenant of salt indicates an agreement that stands for a very long time. It is a very strong one, though it may not be everlasting. When the Bible uses this metaphor, God urges us to remain faithful even when circumstances seem to be on the surface. His word stands sure. His name endures forever because He is the same yesterday, today, and forever.

Salt was always used during burnt offerings in the old testament on the altar, which further shows a preservative power even on the altar.

> Leviticus 2:13 "And every oblation of thy meat offering shalt thou season with salt; neither shalt thou suffer the salt of the covenant of thy God to be lacking from thy meat offering: with all thine offerings thou shalt offer salt."

Leviticus 2:13 "You shall season all your grain offerings with salt. You shall not let the salt of your covenant with your God be missing from your grain offering; with all your offerings, you shall offer salt."

Salt was one of the main items often use in the offering because it spoke of purity, preservation, and expense. Every sacrifice offered to God should be pure, should be enduring, and should cost something

CHAPTER FOUR

THE SPIRITUAL POWER OF SALT

From the days of old, salt has been a powerful spiritual weapon, useful for different things, from purification to healing, cleaning, and even domestically. Salt spiritually talks about a new beginning and been separated from the past. Elisha using salt for purification didn't just show healing but newness; curses and corruption were over, and everything became new.

Several people recognized salt for its various healing properties and its functions both inside the body and outside. The significance of salt has been adored for several thousands of years. Hippocrates recognized that many fishers damaged their hands, and after exposing them- selves to seawater, they ended up not having any infection. He wondered what happened on such occasions, not know- ing it's the seawater with a salt content level and helping to prevent germs from entering through these wounds.

We believe that salt signifies tastiness as nothing can taste better without salt; this is the reason why traditionally; salt the elders use salt to declare over someone, especially during formal events and occa- sions. On many traditional occasions, salt is one of the most important things they use because they recognize its value.

It is one of the essential things demanded during the traditional wedding, especially in Africa and some parts of South Ameri- ca, because of its significance. So much value is attached to it, and without it on such occasions, it is believed such life will lack sweetness. So, it is always written on top of the items to buy for such circumstances.

Besides, traditional worshippers often use salt in their sacrificial offerings to their deities. We believe that a teaspoon of salt is a tool of restoring sweetness to every bad situation or bringing out sweetness, wealth, blessings in a man's life when used. They prepare salt with different varieties before using it.

Job 39:5-6

> "Who sent out the wild donkey freely? And who lose the bonds of the swift donkey, whom I gave the wilderness for a home, and the salt land for his habitation?"

It clearly shows how significant salt is in the life of a man. A salted land for the dwelling is a fruitful land that makes the heart glad. If a man lives in a land devoid of salt, it signifies futility, fruitlessness, and a wilderness experience.

Also, when newborn babies are to be christened, in a traditional way, a little salt is placed in the baby's tongue, and several prayers are said. Words are declared on the baby, further revealing its symbolism of sweetness in an individual's life. Many people have taken this further to apply salts in spiritual ways. Salt has a myriad of functions in different areas of life and not just spiritually.

The Roman Catholic Church, has also mentioned the importance of salt. The 1962 Rituale Romanum added salt in one of the components in the three rites.

Baptism: It was an act often practiced back in those days among the Roman Catholics. Before a person enters the church, they blessed the salt and put a little of it in his mouth to sanctify him. Today, many of them skip the process.

Altar reconsecration: In one of the rites for the altar reconsecration, salt is blessed; ashes, wine, and water mixed with it, and the mixture is used to build the mortar to reseal the temple.

Holy water: Salt is used with holy water and blessed. The blessings invoke the higher powers to take action depending on what your prayer requests are.

CHAPTER FIVE

HEALING POWER OF SALT

Salt acts as a neutralizer because it reduces the body's acidic content, leading to several life-threatening illnesses. Any abnormal increase in the body's pH level can be too acidic or too alkaline and severely negatively affect the body. The balance must be maintained in the body.

A sister I know stopped taking carbohydrates due to menstrual cramps in her early teens, and as a result, began to experience some strange things she didn't understand. Then her system began to shut down on its own. One day she collapsed and was taken to the hospital where it was said that her glucose level was low; that was why her system shut down because her brain was not getting enough glucose.

This is what happened to us when we have an imbalance of hormonal productions or imbalance chemical reactions going on in the body.

The colon cleanses, often called the salt water flush, aid digestion by helping our digestive system. It flushes the unwanted content forcefully out of the colon to prevent unwanted material from staying in the colon to prevent colon cancer issues.

Rock salt possesses healing features. It is mostly used in Ayurvedic medicines and also helps the heart. It helps prevent osteoporosis, decreases depression and stress, helps block off muscle cramps, and can heal it.

It helps heal numbness and tingling sensations, which generally occur due to a lack of proper blood flow to some vital blood vessels. It is believed that salt aids blow circulation and, as such, prevents every disease associated with improper flow of blood through the blood.

Salt is mostly used to stop the flow of blood in fresh wounds. It is funny, but it works when applied to fresh-cut. Aside from the fact that it speeds up the injury's healing process, it also prevents germs from invading the wound, leading to several diseases. It is said to have constriction power on the blood vessels and, as such, stops the bleeding process.

When salt is applied to burns as first aid, it prevents blisters' formation on the area. Water mostly accumulates together when one has burn accidents, which may be very painful. Salt helps to stop the accumulation of this water and also hastens the healing process.

Salt has excellent healing properties that should never be overlooked. It's incredible how a little thing like salt can have such tremendous power both physically and spiritually.

Although salt is powerful in historical and metaphorical terms, many do not pay attention to salt's spiritual use. Spiritually, it is considered a great purifying agent and help to balance up energy while discharging negative thoughts into the surrounding.

Everything around us has energy, and it discharges. People, plants, and animals; the environment we live and breathe is made up of energy.

When you understand the prophetic power of salt, its application becomes easy, and getting what you need becomes effortless as well. Elisha, Elijah's spiritual son, had just received Elijah's mantle, and he was confronted with a territorial problem of corruption and lack of productivity. The spirit of lawlessness had taken over their water, and the land had been desolated; nothing good could come out of that land.

They approached Elisha, the prophet who understood prophetic instructions and principles. "The men of the city told Elisha, "Look, our Lord, this town is well situated, but our water is bad, and the land is unproductive. "Bring me a new bowl and put the salt in it." They brought it to him. He left for the spring, threw the salt in it, and said, "This is what the LORD says 'I have healed the water. Never again will it bring death or make the land unproductive.'" And the water has remained wholesome to this day, according to the word Elisha had spoken. (2 Kings 2:19-22).

The link between their lack of productivity and the desired results was a prophetic instruction. Using salt in prayers is beyond using just salt. It is a prophetic instruction, and every prophetic teaching, when followed, always birth results.

All Elisha needed to do was to pour the salt in a bowl and pour it into the spring, and the spring would be purified; the entire territory was made whole after Elisha carried out the spiritual instruction that was ministered to him.

Most times, what should put an end to our misery and difficulties are just little things like salt that we have ignored for a long time. Elisha did not only heal the land, but he also purified it completely and activated its productivity, and it remains so till today.

CHAPTER SIX

HOW TO USE SALT TO GET WHAT YOU WANT

The different meanings of salt from the scriptures show the level of possibilities is attached to its use. It is very crucial to know how to use it in prayers to gain access to every one of these possibilities. Salt can be applied in different ways.

Giving alms

There are different ways to apply salt in prayers and get answers. Many denominations have different methods of application. Some give salt as alms, especially after some level of consecration and fasting and prayers for a certain number of days, and need to round up the fasting exercises. They are giving salt as alms to speed up answers.

Placing on the altar

Another method of using salt in prayers is blessing the salt, making your requests on the salt after doing every other requirement, and leaving the salt at the prayer altar, especially on the mountain.

A man had prayed for me in a season of my life; the season was full of turmoil, confusion, and weariness. One of the instructions was to pray on salt, bring it to the mountain, drop it there with coconut and light candles, and pray.

Several testimonies have been recorded from instructions attached with salt today, and indifferent churches, even the head give instructions related to salt. A grain of salt is indeed a powerful tool that anyone can use depending on your level of belief.

Salt Bath

Another way to use salt in prayers is to put it in water and bath with it at a specific time, especially if someone is experiencing rejection, setbacks, bad luck, and poverty. It is believed that once you bless the salt, mix with water, and bathe with it, you begin to experience breakthrough, affluence, and things will fall back in shape.

When you mix rock salt with camphor every day and say your daily rituals, and in the evening while the sun is setting, you pour the salt in an aroma oil dispenser, placed at the center of your room. The fragrance will spread to every corner of your room. This attracts wealth to you, good luck, and also activates your guardian angels as they walk with you in life.

Combine camphor with rock salt in a bowl put at every corner of your house. Ensure you change this daily for at least 40 days. This will repel negative energies been discharged into your home and de-activate the work of darkness in your vicinity. The presence of negative energy can be seen in the events happening in your house, your thoughts, and every-thing that is happening. Prolonged misunderstanding, loss of different things for a lengthy time can result from negative energy around your home.

When you allow the salt to stay for 30-40 days, it acts as a magnet and removes every negative energy that may be lurking around your house. Have it in mind that this particular salt is not for food, neither is it for consumption, so ensure it is well kept that your pets will not have any chance to touch or leak it for any reason or trample on it. Dispose after use or when it has stuck together due to its ex-posure to air. Sometimes salt may become watery when exposed to too much breeze. More so, you don't want it permanently at that corner; you should dispose of it when its job is done.

Pick a new packet of salt and put it in your bathroom to be used after every bath. Pick little salt, rub it on your body, forehead, and toe and leave it for few minutes. After a few minutes, rinse off repeat this every time you have your bath. This will prevent negative thoughts and energies to get into you. Do it for 30-40 days. It is a powerful way to sustain positivity.

Rock salt can also be dissolved in the water early in the to clean your body system. It helps to cleanse the body's internal structure. Fill a glass cup with warm water, put two spoonfuls of salt and declare the name of the Lord in it and drink. This is also relevant for stopping stomach ache. When salt is mixed with warm water and drank, it calms down your stomach, which is the end of the stomach pain.

The truth is many things we use salt for are what we learned and heard from the elders. Many people don't believe in doing anything not seen directly in the Bible. But as natural stuff, salt works diversely to heal different sicknesses and illnesses.

Saltwater that has blessed can be used to chase evil spirits away from the house, office, business, etc. this is why many pastors ask their members always to have prayer water in the house and also give instructions to mix with salt and sprinkle it around their home, workplace and even business places.

The devil will do anything to ensure he stops people's blessings, prevent them from living quality lives by attacking them in different ways through sickness, poverty, and every work of darkness. Ignorance is one weapon the devil uses. If you know what to do, then you are free from the devil.

Nightmares can be frightening, and disturbing especially if it persists for a very long time. Black salt can be used to control a nightmare. Salt should be sprinkled in the water stating your desires and intentions are making declarations and saying prayer words. Then bath with it at night before going to bed.

Sprinkling salt

Saltwater should be sprinkled at every corner of your home and office continuously for eight days or can also be done once every month. Only salt sprinkle around the corners of your is enough to chase evil spirit away from your arena. Simply bless the salt, declare the word of peace, and sprinkle, and that is all.

Aside from using water together with salt for prayers, some use other things like honey and oil. There are several instances where not just salt and water will be required for the prayer process, but other items may be involved.

Carrying a covered packet of salt was believed to provide a level of spiritual protection against the world's wickedness as well. Another talisman method used to fight off demonic agents is when a bottle of salt and a knife are used spiritually.

Some people often place salt and pepper in their boots, especially the left boot, for good fortune. For security against the wicked witch, a laborer might throw salt outside the front door and lean a broom next to it.

Note

The best time to do this salt ritual is on the first day of the New Moon. This phase is unique because it marks new beginnings. The chances of success are higher on this day than any other day.

If not, do it on the first Sunday of each month; it works to cleanse the bad energies around us that do not allow us prosper.

RITUAL RECIPES USING SALT

Spiritual Cleansing Salt Bath

This ritual is effective in getting rid of stagnation, negativity, and any burden. These problems weigh you down, making it difficult for you to progress in several areas in your life. To live a healthier, more progressive life, you need to try this relaxing and healing spiritual bath.

INGREDIENTS

salt

lavender essential oil

DIRECTIONS

Fill the tub with hot water, do not add soap or anything

Add a cup of salt

Add 7 drops of lavender essential oil and Swish to mix and dissolve the salt

Relax and soak in the water for 30 minutes

Chant this prayer as many times as you want for spiritual cleansing:

"I call on the healing angels to cleanse me of any negative energy in my life"

"As salt is dissolved inside water, I dissolve all negative energies in me"

"I fill myself with everything positive, progressive and good"

"so shall it be"

Visualize all your problems, dissolving, vanishing and disappearing.

Finish and get out of the tub. Don't towel your body. Air dry!

Salt ritual for financial prosperity

This ritual helps to attract good luck in abundance and success; you can use it for your career, work, business, or money problems. Closed doors are sure to open for you after this ritual.

INGREDIENTS

A white candle

7 dried or fresh red rose petals

Salt

Incense

Dish

DIRECTIONS

Place the plate on your altar.

Use a handful of salt to make a circle on the dish.

Place 7 petals of a red rose on top of the circle of salt.

In the middle of the dish, light a white candle.

Light an incense on your altar

Sit, breathe slowly, and relax. Visualize every path in your life clearing and all the financial doors opening for you.

Then, say this chant out loud:

"I am thankful to my higher self for my success, abundance and prosperity"

"I am rich, divine wealth flows through me"

"I open myself to more financial opportunities"

"So shall it be"

Do this for seven days, repeat this same ritual

Spiritual salt Cleanse for protection

Use this salt ritual for protection; to clear any evil spirits or bad energies from your life, home, and office as often as you need to. It will also promote good finances.

INGREDIENTS

salt

Broom

DIRECTIONS

Clean your floor using a broom to sweep before the spiritual salt cleanse.

Take a handful of salt and place it on the floor.

Using the broom, sweep the salt all over the room.as you repeat the following chant:

"As I sweep this uncountable salt with my broom, I send all evil spirits, no matter the number out of my room, out of my life."

Afterward, collect all the salt and throw it in the toilet bowl, telling water to take away all negativity in your home, in your life.

A Prayer to St. Cajetan with Salt and Candle for Money Rain

In this ritual, we ask a saint for his intercession. Because they are holy saints already living in Heaven, their generous prayers strengthen ours. Start this ritual on a Sunday morning, It's really simple and very effective. Through prayer, you will make a simple request so that money rains upon you. If you don't have an amulet, stamp, or image of St Cajetan, find one online and print it.

INGREDIENTS

Salt

1 image or Prayer card to Saint Cajetan

1 white candle

A cup

DIRECTIONS

Fill the cup with salt and place it on your altar.

Place the image of St. Cajetan inside the cup so that part of it is touching the salt.

Light the white candle.

Focus on the image of the Saint for a minute, cross yourself and say the following prayer:

"O glorious St. Cajetan, you helped the many unemployed people of your time, provided loans without interest and you attracted a lot of benefactors who donated to your resources so that you could go on with your activities. Look on me with mercy. I wish to find that employment, business and abundance to make money fall on me so that i can help me and my family live with dignity. Listen to my pe-

tition, dear saint; you, who could easily give up the food on your table for the needy, bring my petition to Jesus (here make your request). Amen."

Let the candle burn all the way without leaving the room.

Keep the image of Saint Cajetan in your wallet, along with a pinch of salt. Throw away the rest of the salt and the remains of candle wax.

CHAPTER SEVEN

HOW TO BLESS SALT TO GET WHAT YOU WANT

In Christianity, you should know that whatever will attract the face of God must be blessed, and these blessings are what will activate angels to act on your behalf. We can see everywhere in the scripture the roles of angels in bring answered prayers to the saints.

Different denominations in the church have different ways of applying salt in prayers and different ways of blessing salt before using it. Some members will have to meet their spiritual head or pastor to bless the salt, while others do that without consultation. More so, depending on the situation, you can either pray on it yourself or contact someone higher than you in faith.

Simple prayers can be said on the salt by declaring the words of faith or scriptures on the salt. Note that faith is powerful when engaging salt in prayers; without trust, getting what you want may be difficult, sometimes delayed till you can encounter God by faith.
Hebrews 11: 6

"without faith, it is impossible to please God."

Many people do certain things spiritually and still do not get what they want in prayers because they do not engage with faith. It is the reason they often think that it is not potent enough. It is their lack of confidence.

Different people in the various denominations have used salt to get whatever they want in prayers. Some use it with water, candles, and other things and get everything they want in prayers.

Prayers of faith work wonders and should never be trivialized. It is believed that angels wait on your words and act accordingly.

The first method of blessing salt by simply declaring words from the scripture, simply locate every verse of the scripture that speaks about the situation you are in or the kind of results you desire and proclaim these scriptures on the salt and apply it following instructions.

Several scriptures speak about different prayer requests that can be applied, but many are ignorant of scriptural declaration's potency. Instructions can come by impression or inspiration through the Holy ghost or someone else.

The second way of blessing salt by saying a short prayer over the salt

"Lord we ask that you bless this salt,
sanctify it by your blood and let it grant
all my request in Jesus name."

as short as that is, it has tremendous
power in turning things around for your
sake. James 5:16b

> "... the effectual prayer of the righteous
> availeth much"

that is the power of prayer whether short
or long.

One thing you must be mindful of when
believing God to give you all you want is
"The name of Jesus is a strong tower, the
righteous runs in and they are saved"
Proverbs 18: 10. Many battles have been
won by calling this name. Its potency
cannot be overemphasized in Christen-
dom.

CHAPTER EIGHT

FOUR THINGS YOU MUST DO TO GET WHAT YOU WANT IN PRAYERS

Many people miss the answers to their prayers either because they lack knowledge or lack of discernment. When you feel your efforts are in vain and your prayers have not been answered, it can genuinely lead to frustration and the feeling of misery.

Many miss the answers to their prayers because they don't have precise desires or prayer points before starting the blessing and the whole process. One of the keys to answering prayers is being specific.

Specificity:

Being specific in prayers is very powerful. When you know what you want and what exactly you are praying for, your problems are halfway solved before the whole process. Clarity is the ability to separate your questions one by one and find solutions to them after the other. Be specific about your issues to get a definite answer to the problems.

Instructions:

Instructions are the backbone of everything a man tries to build in life. If you are given instructions, follow them till the end. Sometimes, you will be asked to read certain scriptures or perform certain rituals on the salt for days before using the it for any purpose for which it is designed. Ensure you follow every instruction if you desire to get what you want in prayers.

Patience:

Patience is essential when you have carried out every instruction. Lack of patience is what has led to many aborting their promises of God to them in life. Be patient with the process, be patient with God, and you will get everything you desire to get.

Carry someone along:

Except you have been using salt consistently to get the things you want in prayer; ensure you carry a spiritual leader along if you can. This will encourage your heart in case the answers are not forthcoming. Sometimes it is good to fight with others and not fight alone. Involve family and friends where necessary and if part of the instruction is to be secretive about it, then obey.

Gratitude:

This is the key that gets heaven to act on your behalf. No matter what you are trusting God for, be thankful for the process and for what God is set to do. Thanksgiving is mighty when engaged; let it be your lifestyle, and employ it often.

CHAPTER NINE

FOUR SIGNS THAT YOUR PRAYERS HAVE BEEN ANSWERED

There are pointers to answered prayers, and you can only know them when you are clear with what you want from praying with salt. Salt can be used in devotions to get different results and can be applied in different ways.

Applying it when searching for jobs is different from using it when praying for a breakthrough, praying in a formal event, and so on. You must be clear about what you want to know when your answers have arrived.

1. **Breakthrough**: If you have been struggling with stagnancy and praying for a breakthrough, things begin to work out for you suddenly. You begin to receive responses from places you never expected. This is peculiar with issues like this.

2. **Restoration:** Many people desire restoration, mostly when they have lost a lot in businesses and life. When salt is used in praying for restoration, you will begin to see different happenings that will cause you to experience miraculous shifts.

   Things that you lost are restored; sometimes speed is peculiar to repair; it is a way God restore stuff to people, either speed in business to get double of what they lost or speed in marriage to get a double portion of everything they lost.

3. **Ease:** One of the major signs of answered prayer is ease. Salt sometimes is used in declaring comfort to one's life in prayers, and when the prayer is answered, things become easy for the individual.

4. **Joyfulness:** your life is full of gratitude as situations begin to change for good. Being joyful doesn't mean you have an apparent reason, but because the internal turmoil is over and your hope is alive, things will fall back into pleasant places. Salt means sweetness, and one way it brings sweetness is by bringing joy and happiness when used in prayers.

No man can deny the potency of salt in getting what you desire in prayers. When used right, it breaks stagnancy and causes you to experience a breakthrough in diverse ways that we can't explain.

Made in the USA
Thornton, CO
10/22/24 11:08:39